Crafts for Christian Values

Crafts
for
Christian
Values

By Kathy Ross

Illustrated by Sharon Lane Holm

The Millbrook Press   Brookfield, Connecticut

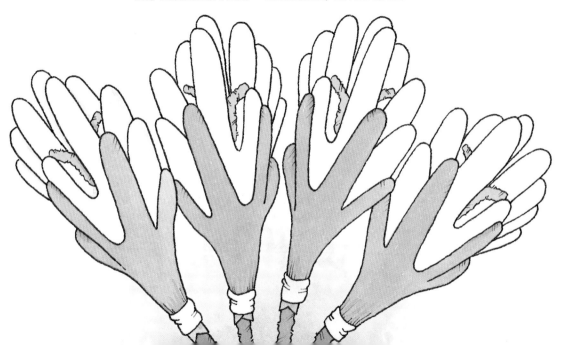

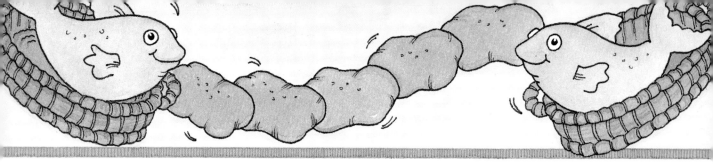

For my best friend ever, Bev
K.R.

For Lovely Linda
S.L.H.

With thanks to Patti M. Hummel and the Benchmark Group
for their assistance in the preparation of this book.

Library of Congress Cataloging -in-Publication Data
Ross, Kathy (Katharine Reynolds), 1948-
Crafts for Christian values / by Kathy Ross ; illustrated by Sharon Lane Holm.
p. cm.
ISBN 0-7613-1618-3 (lib. bdg.) — ISBN 0-7613-1284-6 (pbk.)
1. Bible crafts. 2. Values—Study and teaching. 3. Christian education of children.
I. Holm, Sharon Lane. II. Title.
BS613.R66 2000   268'.432—dc21   00-021805

Published by The Millbrook Press, Inc.
2 Old New Milford Road
Brookfield, Connecticut 06804
www.millbrookpress.com

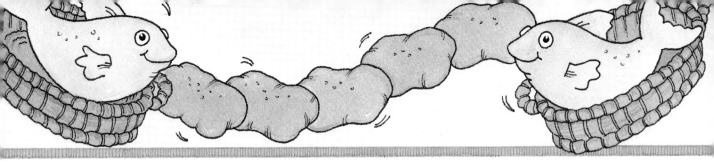

Contents

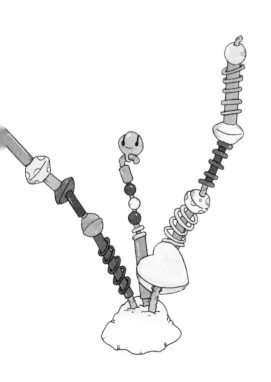

Introduction

Dear Crafters,

I have always been a hands-on learner. My understanding of not only things, but also ideas increases when I am an active participant in the learning process. I suspect the same to be true for many children. Adults can explain to children the kinds of behavior God wants from us, but often children are not sure how to go about practicing such behavior. They need models.

And so, I wrote this book to help children learn about Christian values. I have designed a collection of craft activities that direct and encourage children in practicing values in a very concrete way. The child can make a stabile to keep track of church attendance, record and remember the kindness of others with a gratitude jar, and make a mustard seed necklace as a reminder of the power of faith.

These easy-to-make projects, coupled with more structured curriculum programs that teach children the importance of living by Christian values, will serve as an enhancement to home learning.

Kathy Ross

Keep a loving heart.

Loving Heart Beanbag

red
pom-pom

old pink or red sock

red yarn

two wiggle eyes

thin red ribbon

scissors

stapler

white glue

pencil

dry
red beans

what you do:

1 Cut off the foot of the sock about 5 inches (13 cm) from the toe end. Trim the cut end to form two bumps to look like the top of a heart.

2 Turn the sock inside out. Starting at the center of the toe, staple the two sides of the sock into a point to form the bottom of the heart. Turn the sock right-side out.

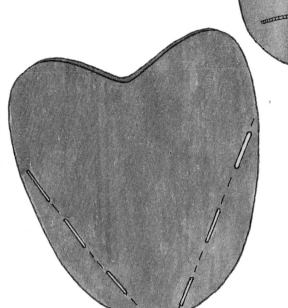

3 Glue the front and back of the heart together, leaving an opening between the two bumps just large enough to slip a bean through.

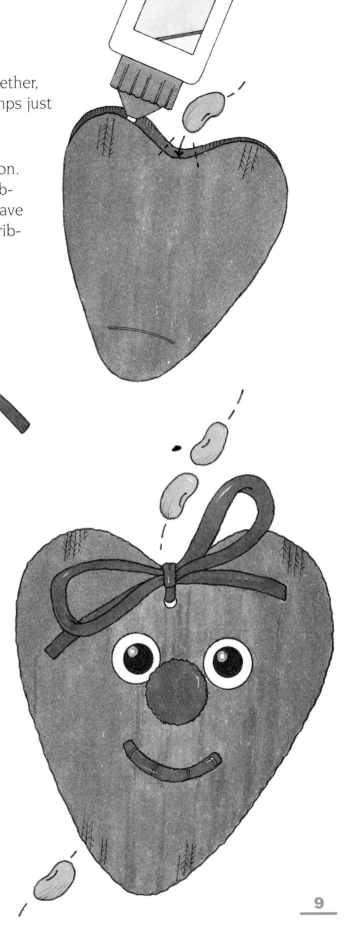

4 Cut a 10-inch (25-cm) length of red ribbon. Use the pencil to push one end of the ribbon through the front and back of the sock weave at the opening at the top of the heart. Tie the ribbon in a bow to close the opening.

5

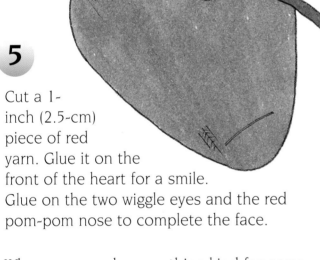

Cut a 1-inch (2.5-cm) piece of red yarn. Glue it on the front of the heart for a smile. Glue on the two wiggle eyes and the red pom-pom nose to complete the face.

Whenever you do something kind for someone, untie the ribbon and put a bean in your beanbag heart, then tie it closed again. How long will it take you to fill your heart? What a nice way to remember to keep a loving heart!

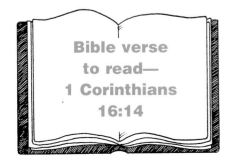

Bible verse
to read—
1 Corinthians
16:14

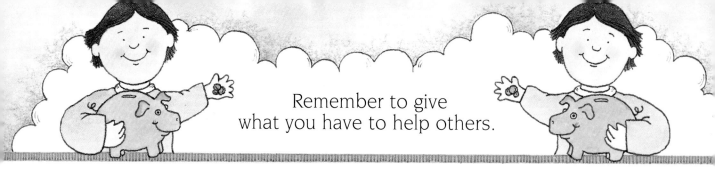
Lamb Mission Bank

you need:

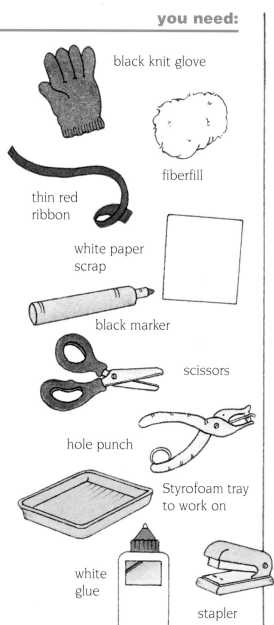

black knit glove

fiberfill

thin red
ribbon

white paper
scrap

black marker

scissors

hole punch

Styrofoam tray
to work on

white
glue

stapler

what you do:

1 Cut a 1-foot (30-cm) length
of red ribbon. Staple one
end to the inside of each side of
the opening of the glove to make
a hanger.

2 Cover the palm and half
the thumb of the
glove with glue, then
cover the glue with
fiberfill. Turn the glove
over and do the same
thing on the other side.

This will be the
body of the
sheep with the
four fingers
hanging down
for the legs
and the thumb
forming the
head.

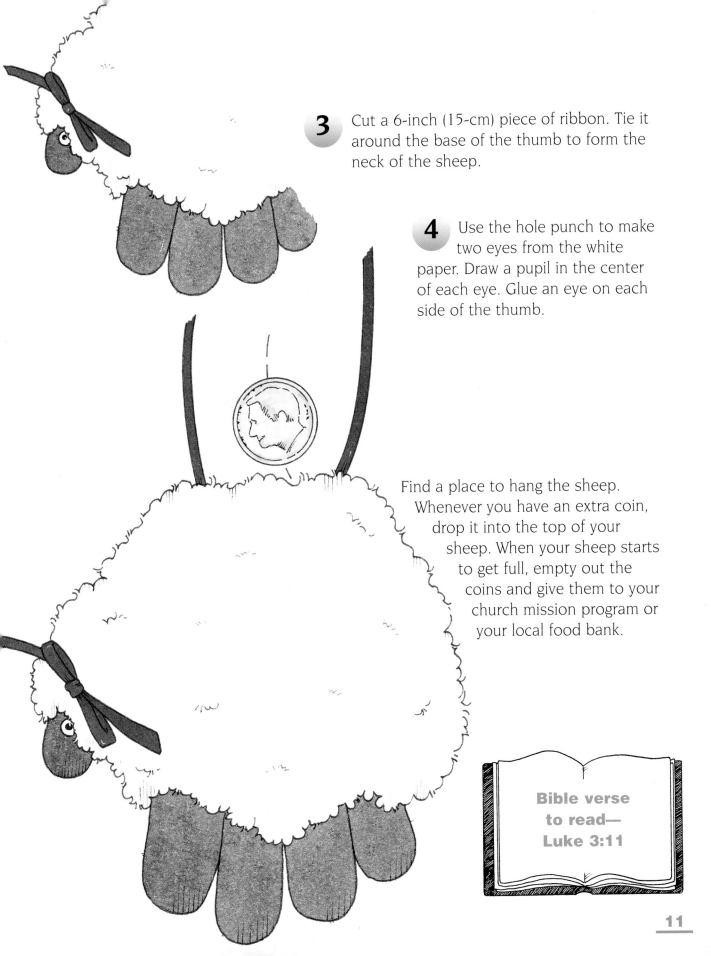

3 Cut a 6-inch (15-cm) piece of ribbon. Tie it around the base of the thumb to form the neck of the sheep.

4 Use the hole punch to make two eyes from the white paper. Draw a pupil in the center of each eye. Glue an eye on each side of the thumb.

Find a place to hang the sheep. Whenever you have an extra coin, drop it into the top of your sheep. When your sheep starts to get full, empty out the coins and give them to your church mission program or your local food bank.

Bible verse to read— Luke 3:11

Be filled with joy!

Joyful Noise Hat

what you do:

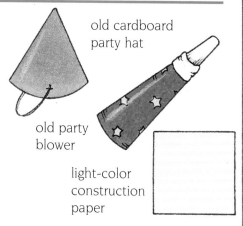
old cardboard party hat

old party blower

light-color construction paper

markers

scissors

white glue

masking tape

stickers

1 Carefully unglue the seam of the hat and flatten it to use as a pattern. Use a marker to trace around the hat on the construction paper. Cut the hat shape out.

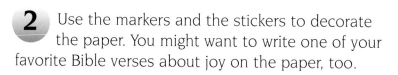

2 Use the markers and the stickers to decorate the paper. You might want to write one of your favorite Bible verses about joy on the paper, too.

Make a Joyful Noise to the Lord all the Earth. palsm 98.4

3 Glue the paper over the cardboard hat. Glue the seam of the hat back together.

4 Cut the cardboard part off the party blower so that you only have the plastic blower from the end.

5 Cut just enough off the point of the hat so that the cut end of the blower will fit down through the hole. Use the masking tape to hold the blower in place inside the hat. The end you blow into should stick out from the top of the hat.

When you wear your "joyful" hat you will be ready to make a joyful noise by taking the hat off and blowing on the horn.

Bible verse
to read
Psalm 100:
1–2

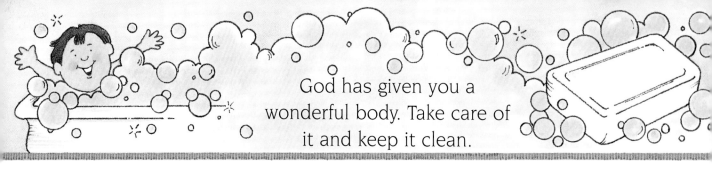

God has given you a wonderful body. Take care of it and keep it clean.

Soap Surprise

bar of mild white soap

grater

small dish

tablespoon

two small surprises— a coin, plastic figure, or 1-inch (2.5-cm) ball

Styrofoam egg carton

what you do:

1 Grate the soap over a dish. You do not need to grate the entire bar. Stop when it gets hard to hold onto, which is about three-fourths of the bar. If you are very young, you will need to ask an adult to do this part for you.

2 Add about 1 tablespoon of water to the soap and mix it in so that the soap sticks together again. You may need to add a bit more water, but do this in very tiny amounts or it will be mushy and hard to shape.

3 You will have enough to make two soap balls. Shape half the mixture in a ball around each surprise. Let the soap balls air-dry overnight on an opened Styrofoam egg carton.

This project is fun to do with a friend. You can each find a special surprise and make a soap ball for each other. You will have to wash your hands a lot to find out what is inside!

Bible verse
to read—
Isaiah 1:16

Perseverance is when you keep trying,
even when something is difficult.

Accomplishment Pencil Can

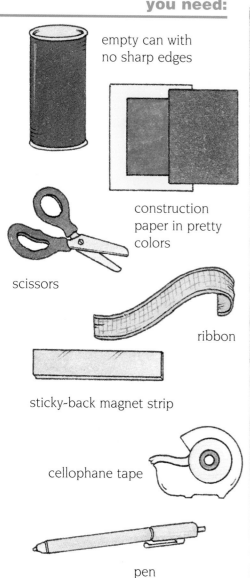

you need:

empty can with
no sharp edges

construction
paper in pretty
colors

scissors

ribbon

sticky-back magnet strip

cellophane tape

pen

what you do:

1 Cut a strip of construction paper
to fit around the can to cover it. Tape
the paper in place around the can.

2 Tie a pretty ribbon around the top of
the can.

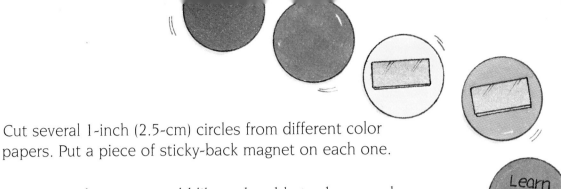

3 Cut several 1-inch (2.5-cm) circles from different color papers. Put a piece of sticky-back magnet on each one.

4 Write something you would like to be able to do on each circle. Stick the circles with things you would like to accomplish around the outside of the can. Once you have accomplished something, move the circle into the inside of the can, and make a circle for something new you would like to achieve.

Keep the accomplishment can on your desk for your pencils and pens. It will serve as a reminder to work hard at being the person that God wants you to be.

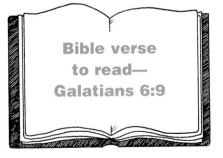

Learn to play the piano

Learn the 23rd Psalm

Get a good grade in math.

Learn to set the table

Learn a new Bible story

Make a new friend

Keep my room clean for 1 week

Learn the 23rd psalm

Save $ for mission

Get a good grade in spelling

Get a good grade in math.

Read 1 book a month

Write to Grandma

Save $ for mission

Bible verse to read— Galatians 6:9

Be quiet in

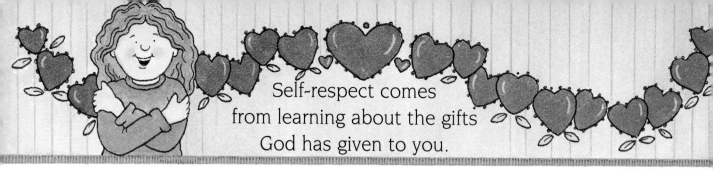

Self-respect comes
from learning about the gifts
God has given to you.

Thoughts Box

you need:

sturdy cardboard box

photo or drawing of you

white glue

markers

pen

pad of sticky notes

what you do:

1 Decorate the lid of the box by gluing a picture of you in the center. Use the markers to write, "I look this way outside of me." You can also add whatever other words and drawings you would like to decorate the lid.

I look this way outside of me.

2 On the inside of the box keep a pen and a pad of sticky notes. Use them to write down your thoughts and feelings, then stick them in the box. You might want to add the date, too.

You will quickly have to layer the thoughts one on top of the other with so many thoughts and feelings going through your head every day. Go through the notes after a few weeks. Did God change your mind about the way you feel about something? Were you concerned about something that turned out fine? Do you wish you felt differently about something? Use your "thoughts box" to draw nearer to God.

Bible verse
to read—
Proverbs 19:8

Honor your parents.

Bottle-Cap Photo Frames

you need:

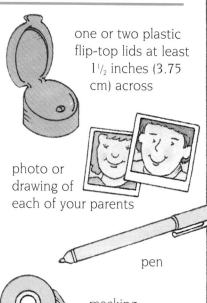

one or two plastic flip-top lids at least 1½ inches (3.75 cm) across

photo or drawing of each of your parents

pen

masking tape

trim

white glue

scissors

what you do:

1 Find or make a small picture of your parent to put in the bottle-cap frame. Center the lid over the face in the photo and trace around the lid with the pen. Cut the picture out.

2 Cut a piece of pretty trim long enough to fit around the outside of the lid.

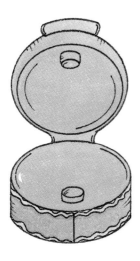

Open the flip-top. Glue the trim around the outside of the lid, overlapping the ends of the trim opposite the flip-top hinge.

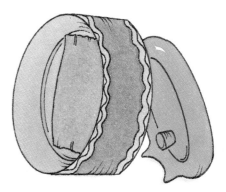

3 Put a piece of masking tape inside the top to create a better gluing surface. Stand your frame up by using the opened top like an easel to prop up the cap picture frame. If you glued a picture of your Mom in the frame, make a second one for your Dad.

Put the little pictures of your Mom and Dad in a place where you can see them often and be reminded of how important they are to you.

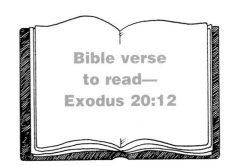

Bible verse to read—
Exodus 20:12

Love your family.

My Family Bookmark

you need:

construction paper

clear wide packing tape

scissors

white glue

small hole punch

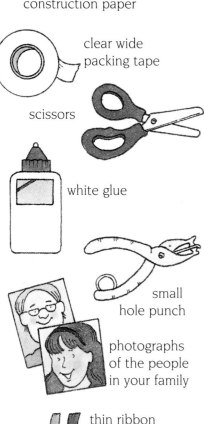

photographs of the people in your family

thin ribbon in two colors

what you do:

1 From the photographs, cut out just the heads of each of your family members. If you have a very small family, use more than one photo of each person. If you do not have any photos for this craft, draw pictures of the head of each family member.

2 Glue the heads on the construction paper to form a long strip. Let the glue dry before continuing.

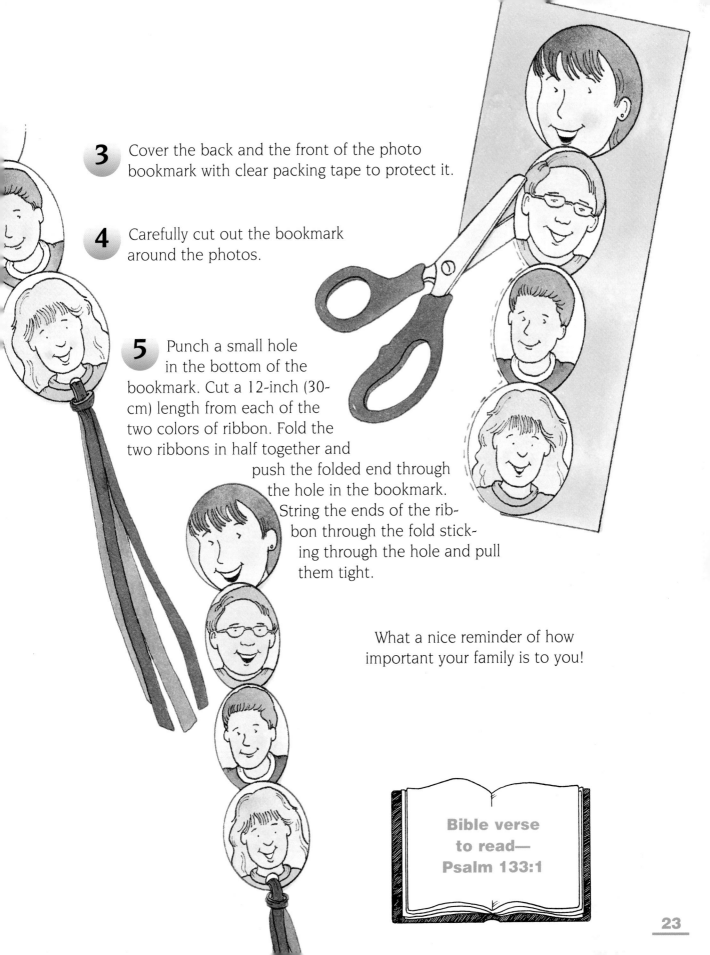

3 Cover the back and the front of the photo bookmark with clear packing tape to protect it.

4 Carefully cut out the bookmark around the photos.

5 Punch a small hole in the bottom of the bookmark. Cut a 12-inch (30-cm) length from each of the two colors of ribbon. Fold the two ribbons in half together and push the folded end through the hole in the bookmark. String the ends of the ribbon through the fold sticking through the hole and pull them tight.

What a nice reminder of how important your family is to you!

Bible verse to read— Psalm 133:1

Be helpful.

Helpful Hand Magnet

you need:

access to a copy machine

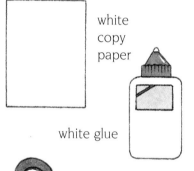

white copy paper

white glue

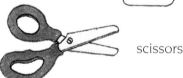

scissors

clear wide packing tape

colorful macaroni craft letters

sticky-back magnet

what you do:

1 Ask an adult to help you copy your hand on a copy machine, then reduce the height of the hand to about 2 inches (5 cm).

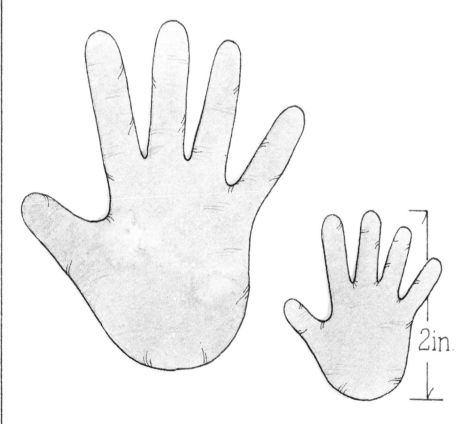

2in.

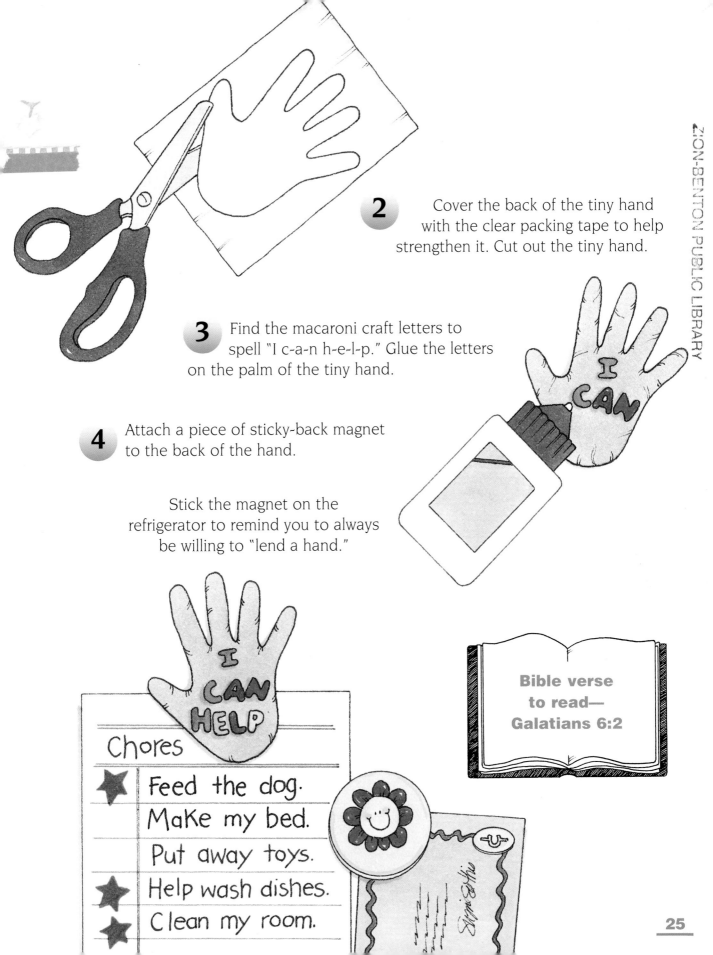

2 Cover the back of the tiny hand with the clear packing tape to help strengthen it. Cut out the tiny hand.

3 Find the macaroni craft letters to spell "I c-a-n h-e-l-p." Glue the letters on the palm of the tiny hand.

4 Attach a piece of sticky-back magnet to the back of the hand.

Stick the magnet on the refrigerator to remind you to always be willing to "lend a hand."

Bible verse to read— Galatians 6:2

Chores

⭐ Feed the dog.
   Make my bed.
   Put away toys.
⭐ Help wash dishes.
⭐ Clean my room.

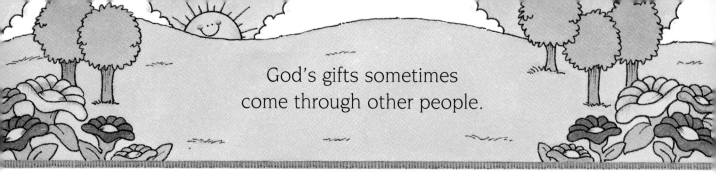

God's gifts sometimes
come through other people.

Gratitude Jar

you need:

large plastic
jar with a
screw-on lid

two buttons

 red pipe cleaner

old colored sock

thin ribbon

red construction
paper

pen

scissors

cellophane tape

paper and pencil

what you do:

1 Soak the jar in warm water to remove the label and glue.

2 Cut a 3-inch (8-cm) heart from the red construction paper. Write "Thank you God for the kindness of others" on the front of the heart. Tape the heart inside the jar so that you can read the words through the plastic jar.

3 Tape the two buttons to the inside top of the jar above the heart to look like eyes.

4 Cut a 1-inch (2.5-cm) piece of pipe cleaner and shape it into a smile. Tape the smile inside the jar just below the eyes.

5 Cut about 4 inches (10 cm) off the cuff of the sock to use for a hat. Cut an 8-inch (20-cm) length of ribbon and tie it around the cut end of the cuff piece to close it. Tie the ribbon in a pretty bow. Put the cuff over the lid of the jar to look like a hat.

6 Keep notepaper and the pencil beside the jar, so you can write down the kind things that others have done for you. Store the notes in your gratitude jar.

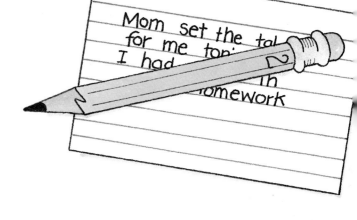

God works through His people. The "gratitude jar" will help you remember the many kindnesses you have received from other people. Maybe you will want to help fill the "gratitude jars" of others!

Bible verse to read— Deuteronomy 8:10

Be responsible by cheerfully doing
the things that are yours to do.

Desk Paper Organizer

you need:

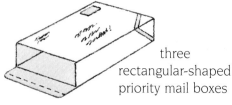

three
rectangular-shaped
priority mail boxes

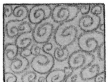

pretty wrapping
paper

white glue

construction paper
in color that blends
well with the wrap-
ping paper

scissors

masking tape

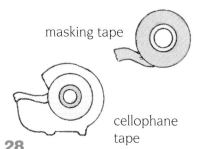

cellophane
tape

what you do:

1 Cut the flaps off one end of each of the priority mail boxes. If the boxes are not already unfolded and sealed at the other end, do this now.

2 Stack the three boxes on top of each other to make the three shelves for the organizer. Glue the boxes together.

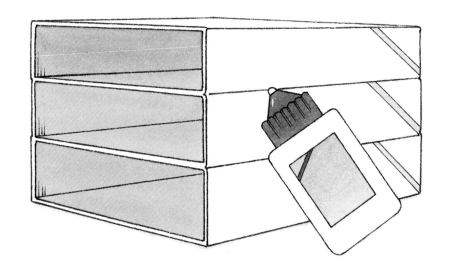

3 Wrap the back and sides of the box in pretty paper just as you would wrap a present, but do not cover up the open end of the boxes. Rub some glue on the boxes under the paper, then hold the paper in place with the cellophane tape.

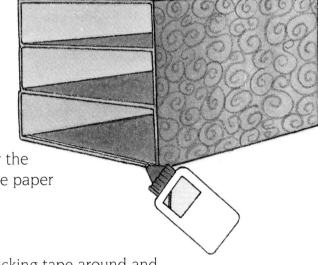

4 Cut a piece of construction paper to cover the bottom of each box compartment. Glue the paper liner on the bottom of each shelf.

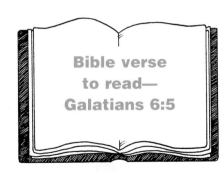

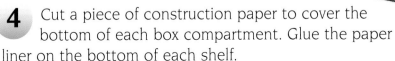

5 Put a strip of masking tape around and across the front edge of each shelf to finish the edges.

Keep the box on your desk to help you organize your papers for school. You might want to label the front of each shelf for different papers, such as "work to do" and "work to hand in."

Bible verse
to read—
Galatians 6:5

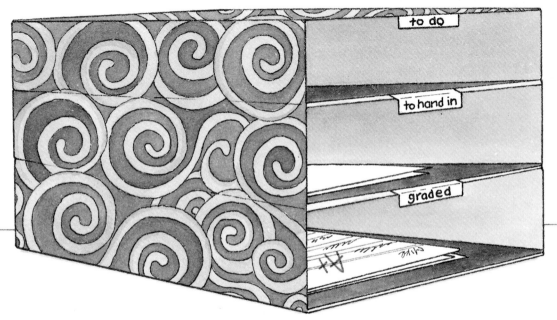

to do

to hand in

graded

Remember
to be thankful for all
that you have been given.

"Thankful for My Food" Book

you need:

14 uncoated white paper plates

hole punch

yarn

scissors

cellophane tape

markers

what you do:

1 Stack two plates on top of each other and punch a series of holes through the rims of both, spaced about 11/2 to 2 inches (4 to 5 cm) apart.

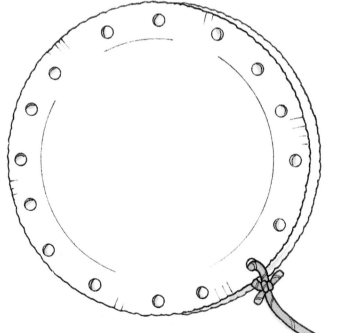

2 Cut a 2-foot (60-cm) length of yarn for each plate. Tie one end of the yarn through a hole in one of the plates. Wrap the other end of the yarn with cellophane tape to make a "needle" to sew with.

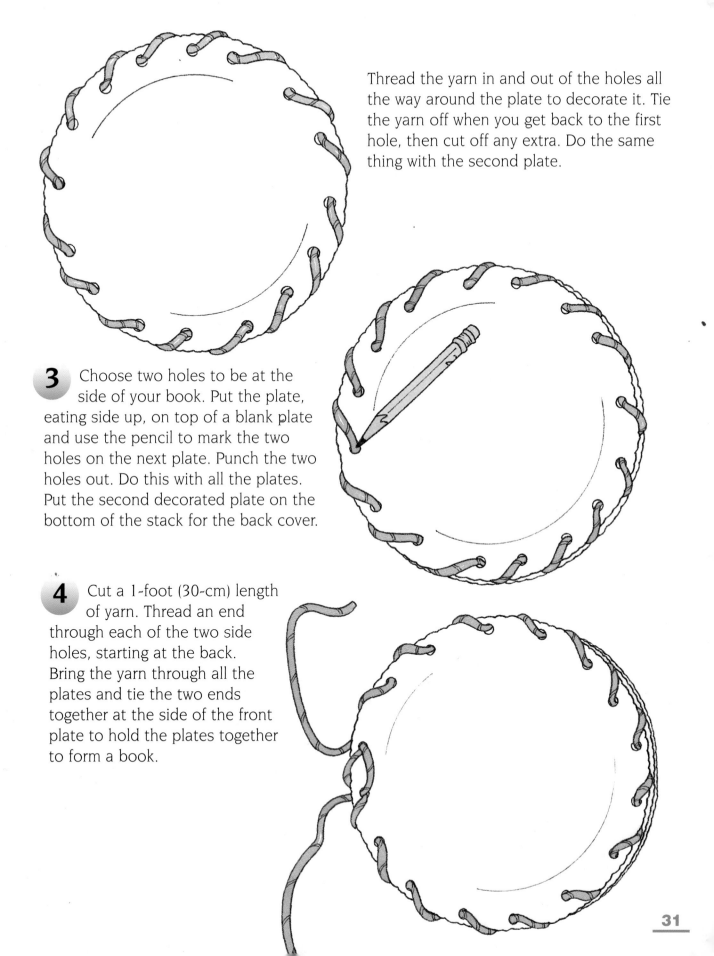

Thread the yarn in and out of the holes all the way around the plate to decorate it. Tie the yarn off when you get back to the first hole, then cut off any extra. Do the same thing with the second plate.

3 Choose two holes to be at the side of your book. Put the plate, eating side up, on top of a blank plate and use the pencil to mark the two holes on the next plate. Punch the two holes out. Do this with all the plates. Put the second decorated plate on the bottom of the stack for the back cover.

4 Cut a 1-foot (30-cm) length of yarn. Thread an end through each of the two side holes, starting at the back. Bring the yarn through all the plates and tie the two ends together at the side of the front plate to hold the plates together to form a book.

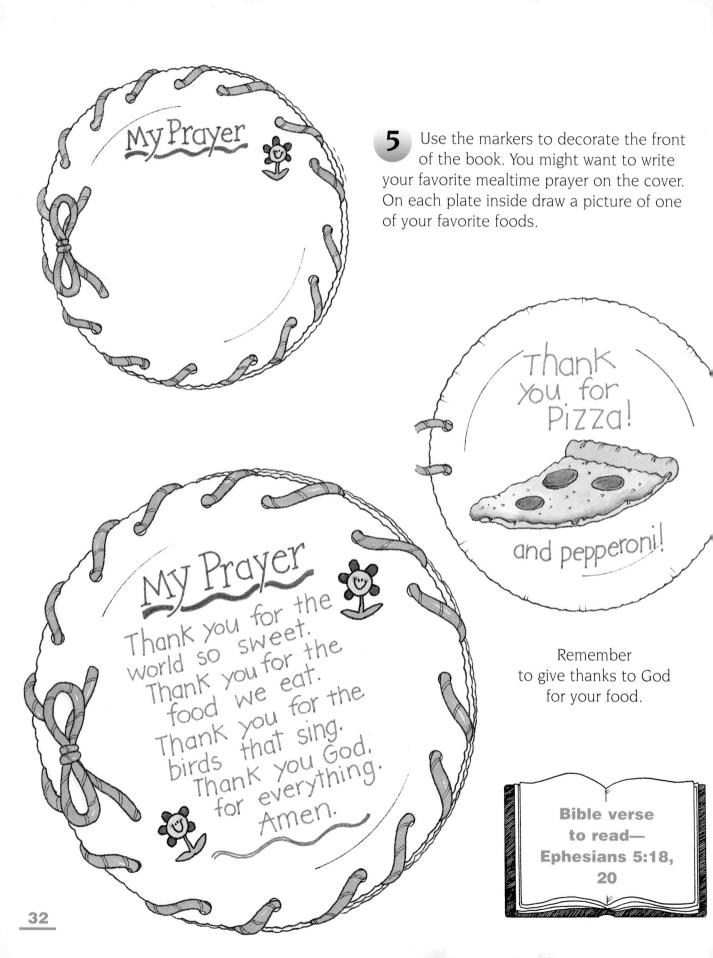

My Prayer

5 Use the markers to decorate the front of the book. You might want to write your favorite mealtime prayer on the cover. On each plate inside draw a picture of one of your favorite foods.

ThanK you for Pizza!

and pepperoni!

Remember to give thanks to God for your food.

My Prayer
Thank you for the world so sweet.
Thank you for the food we eat.
Thank you for the birds that sing.
Thank you God. for everything.
Amen.

Bible verse to read—
Ephesians 5:18, 20

Attend church every week to
worship and learn about God.

Church Attendance Stabile

you need:

clay or
Play-Doh™

pipe cleaners

variety of beads,
buttons, and jingle bells

what you do:

1 Roll a 2-inch (5-cm) ball of clay or Play-Doh™ for the base of the stabile.

2 Cut three pieces of pipe cleaner 4 to 6 inches (10 to 15 cm) long. Stick the ends of the pipe cleaners into the top of the Play-Doh™ ball.

3 Each week that you attend church, choose a bead, button, or bell to string on one of the pipe cleaners.

Add something each week until the stems of the stabile are filled. You might want to keep your stabile at church until it is finished.

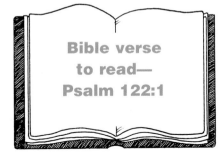

**Bible verse
to read—
Psalm 122:1**

33

Learn the power of prayer.

Prayer Puppet

you need:

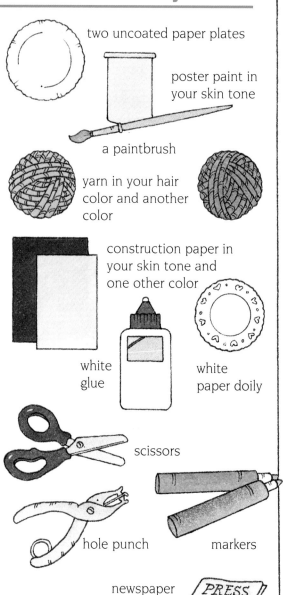

two uncoated paper plates

poster paint in your skin tone

a paintbrush

yarn in your hair color and another color

construction paper in your skin tone and one other color

white glue

white paper doily

scissors

hole punch

markers

newspaper to work on

what you do:

1 Glue the two plates together to make one sturdier plate. Paint the bottom of the combined plate in your skin tone for the face of the puppet. Let the paint dry.

2 Glue on yarn for hair. Draw a face with the markers.

3 Fold two large sheets of construction paper in half lengthwise. Cut the two strips in half to make the front and back of each arm.

4 Fold the skin-colored paper in half. Trace your hand, fingers together, on the folded paper. Cut out the hand on the folded paper so that you have two hands.

front

back

5 Punch a hole in the center of the end of the front paper of each sleeve. Cut two 3-foot (90-cm) lengths of yarn. Thread one end through the front of the hole at the end of each sleeve and glue the end in place behind the front sleeve.

6 Glue the front and back of each arm together with the wrist end of a hand in between the end of each sleeve, palms forward and the thumbs toward the outside.

7 Glue the top ends of each sleeve across each other at an angle. Punch a hole in the center bottom of the two arms where they are glued together.

8 Cut the doilies in half. Glue the two halves on the top of the two sleeves to look like a collar. Glue on the head over the top part of the collar.

9 Thread the ends of the two long pieces of yarn up through the hole in the center of the two arms.

To bring the puppet's hands together in prayer, pull on the two yarn ends hanging down from the back of the puppet.

Bible verse to read—
1 Thessalonians 5:17

Show compassion
by remembering those
who are sick.

Decorated Tissue Box

you need:

unopened box
of tissues

scissors

white
glue

poster
paint

pretty ribbon, trims,
small beads, and
artificial flowers

a paintbrush

newspaper
to work on

Bible verse
to read—
Colossians 3:12

what you do:

1 Paint the outside of the unopened tissue box one
or more pretty colors. Let the paint dry.

2 Decorate the painted box with collage materials.
Do not decorate the part of the box that will be
discarded when the tissue box is opened.

Make a decorated tissue box
to cheer up someone you
know who is sick.

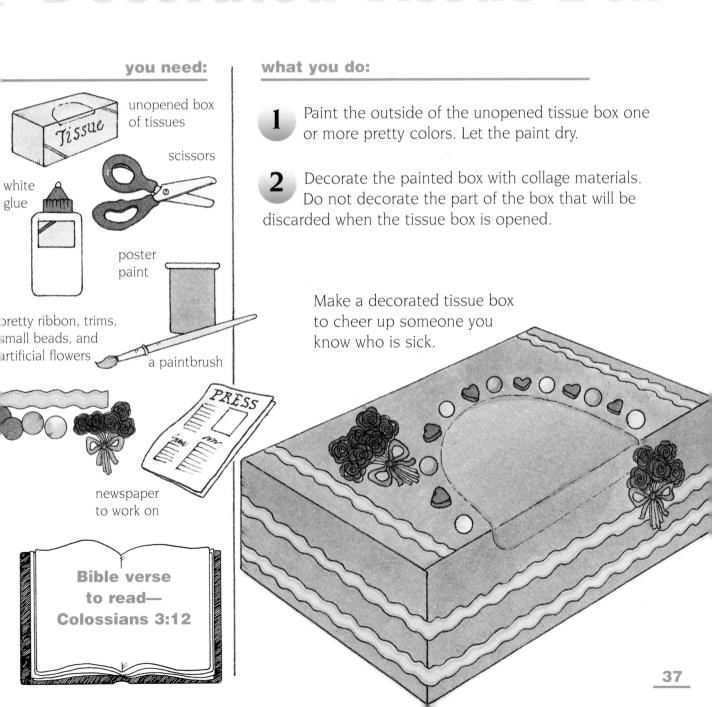

Hear or read
the Bible everyday.

Bible Favorites Bookmark

you need:

white construction
paper

nickel
to trace
around

spool of thin
ribbon

white glue

scissors

pen

what you do:

1 Cut three 2-foot (60-cm) lengths of ribbon.

2 Hold them together and fold them in half. Knot them together about 2 inches (5 cm) down from the fold.

3 Fold the construction paper in half. Use the nickel as a pattern to draw six circles on the white construction paper. Cut each stack of two circles out. Glue each stack of two circles together with the end of one of the ribbons between them. Let the glue dry.

4 Write the book and the chapter and verse numbers of one of your favorite Bible verses on each circle.

Place the marker in your Bible with each ribbon marking one of your favorite verses so you can find it easily.

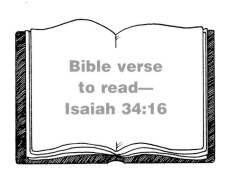

Bible verse to read— Isaiah 34:16

Remember to use good manners.

Good Manners Puppet

you need:

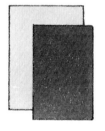
skin-tone and red construction paper

stapler

small pudding box

yarn bits

white glue

masking tape

marker

scissors

what you do:

1 Tape the open end of the box closed. Cut around the front and two sides of the box at the center. Fold the box in half over the uncut side. The box will form a face with the fold being the mouth.

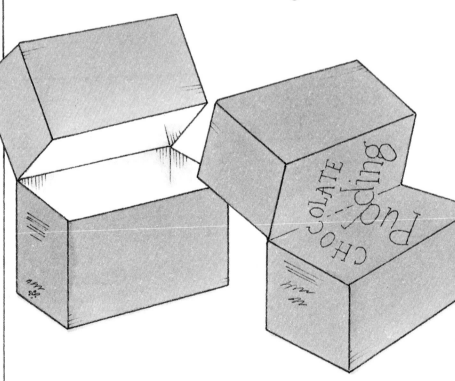

2 Flatten the box and trace around the front on the red paper. Cut the traced shape out. You will need six of this shape to make a little book.

40

3 Stack the six red sheets together and fold them in half to fit inside the folded mouth of the puppet. Staple the papers at the fold to hold them together. Write something polite that a person might say on each page of the book. Glue the book inside the puppet's mouth.

4 Cover the top and bottom parts of the puppet's face with the skin-tone construction paper.

5 Glue yarn bits to the top of the puppet for hair.

6 Use the marker to give the puppet eyes and a nose above the mouth.

This is a very polite puppet!

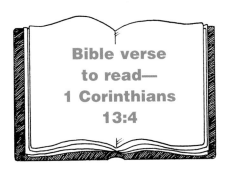

Bible verse to read—
1 Corinthians 13:4

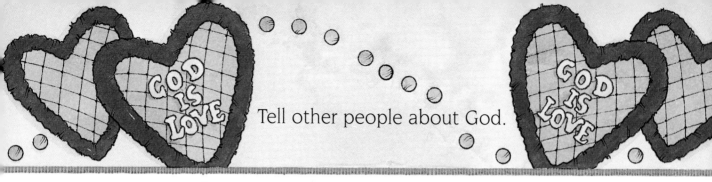
Tell other people about God.

Proclaim God's Word Necklace

you need:

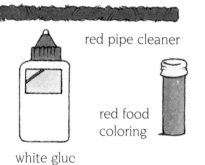

red pipe cleaner

red food coloring

white glue

plastic margarine tub lid

paper cup and craft stick for mixing

yarn

macaroni letters

what you do:

1 Shape the end of the red pipe cleaner into a small heart. Trim off any extra pipe cleaner.

2 Cut a 2-foot (60-cm) length of yarn. Tie the yarn around the top of the heart, then tie the ends of the yarn together to make a necklace.

3 Rub some glue around the back of the pipe-cleaner heart and glue it to the plastic lid.

4 Pour a small amount of glue into the paper cup. Add a drop of red food coloring. Do not add more or the glue will become watery. The glue will dry a much darker shade of red than when it is wet. Mix the color into the glue.

5 Fill the heart with the colored glue. Let dry completely on a flat surface without being disturbed. This could take several days.

6 Find the macaroni letters to spell "God Is Love." Use white glue to glue them to the front of the heart. The glue will be clear when it dries.

Wear your necklace as a reminder to tell others about God.

Bible verse to read— Luke 9:60

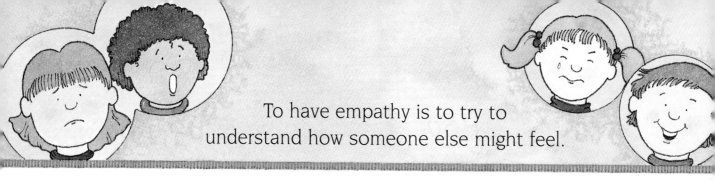

To have empathy is to try to understand how someone else might feel.

Cheerful Cookie Box

you need:

two identical disposable plastic containers with lids

photos, drawings, and old greeting cards

scissors

sticky bow

what you do:

1 Cut a total of four different pictures to fit, with the edges slightly overlapping, around the four sides of one of the containers.

2 Lightly set one container inside the other. Slide the pictures down between the two containers to cover the four sides. Press the inner container down to secure the pictures in place between them.

3 Place a lid on the top container. Stick a sticky bow on the center of the lid.

Fill the container with some yummy cookies and surprise someone who might be feeling sad or lonely.

Bible verse to read—
1 Corinthians 9:22

Recycling is a way of caring for the world that God has given us.

Recycled Crayons

you need:

foil cupcake wrappers

old crayon stubs

zip-to-close
plastic bag

wooden mallet

what you do:

1 Peel the wrappers off several old crayons of similar shades of color.

2 Put the pieces in a zip-to-close plastic bag and seal it, first squeezing out as much air as possible. Gently tap on the crayons with the mallet to break them into smaller pieces. The smaller the crayon bits, the faster they will melt together.

3

Fill a foil muffin cup with crayon pieces about three-quarters full.

4

Put the cup in the hot sun to melt the crayon bits into a big new crayon. If it is too cold to melt the crayons, ask an adult to place the cup in a 250-degree oven on a foil-covered cookie sheet for a few minutes until the crayons melt together.

5 Let the crayon cup air-cool, then pop it out of the foil wrapper.

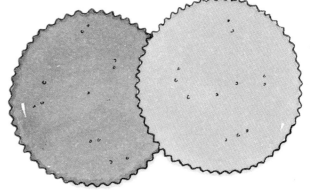

Use old crayons to make lots of new crayons in different shades and colors.

Bible verse to read— Psalm 33:5

God tells us to share what
we have with others.

Loaves and Fishes Pin

you need:

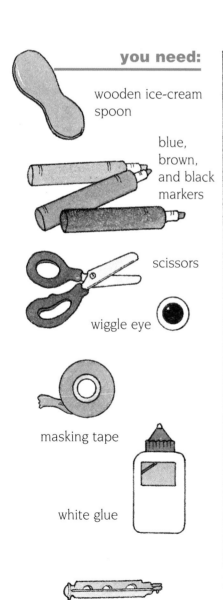

wooden ice-cream
spoon

blue,
brown,
and black
markers

scissors

wiggle eye

masking tape

white glue

safety pin or pin back

what you do:

1 Cut the spoon in half. The larger end of the spoon will be the fish. Trim the cut end to look like the tail of a fish. The smaller half of the spoon will be the loaf of bread. Round off the corners of the cut end.

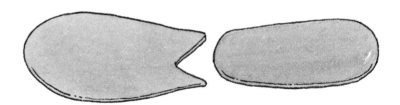

2 Color the fish blue. Use the black marker to add detail such as scales and fins.

3 Put a piece of masking tape on the back of the wiggle eye to create a better gluing surface. Glue the wiggle eye to the head of the fish.

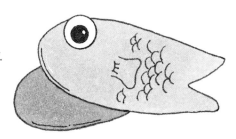

4 Color the loaf of bread with the brown marker.

5 Glue the fish to one side of the loaf of bread so that the bread is still visible.

6 Put a piece of masking tape on the side of the safety pin or pin back that will be glued to the back of the loaf of bread to create a better gluing surface. Glue on the pin back or safety pin and let the glue dry.

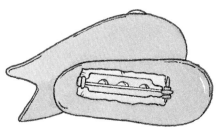

Wear this pin as a reminder of the wonderful miracle that Jesus performed with what one little boy was willing to share (Matthew 14:17–20).

Bible verse to read—
Hebrews 13:16

Be patient in all
you do.

Decorated Pot

you need:

 clay flowerpot

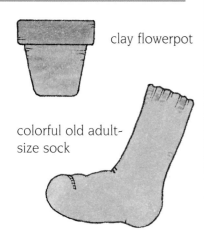 colorful old adult-size sock

two colorful 1-inch (2.5-cm) craft buttons

 12-inch (30-cm) green pipe cleaner

scissors

 masking tape

what you do:

1 Slip the cuff of the sock over the pot to see how much you will need to cover it. Cut off the excess sock. Secure the ends of the sock around the bottom edge of the pot using masking tape. Do not cover up the hole in the bottom of the pot.

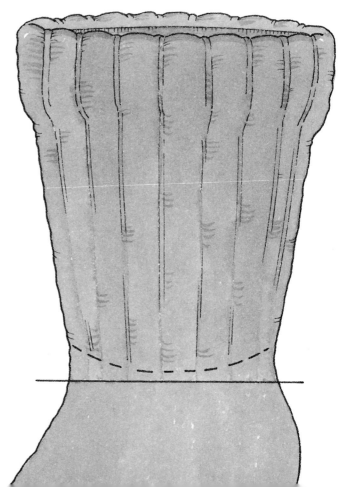

2 Cut the pipe cleaner into four pieces. Stick the end of one piece of pipe cleaner down into the cuff of the sock for a flower stem. Thread the other end in and out of the sock to secure it, then thread a button on the top of the pipe cleaner for a flower.

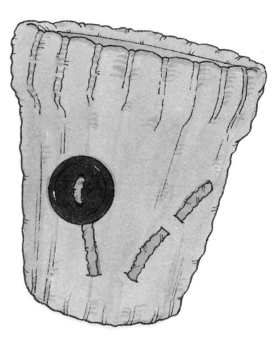

3 Wrap a second piece of pipe cleaner around the center of the stem so that the two ends form leaves for the flower.

4 Make a second flower next to the first one in the same way.

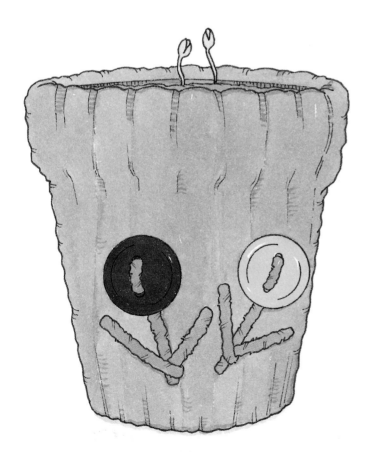

Plant some seeds in the pot and wait patiently for God's miracle.

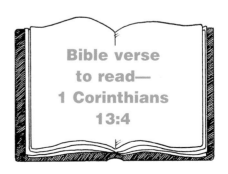

Bible verse to read—
1 Corinthians 13:4

Live your life with courage
knowing God is with you.

Ice Candles

what you do:

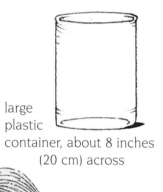

large
plastic
container, about 8 inches
(20 cm) across

water

mittens or gloves
to work with
votive candle

1 Pour about 6 to 8 inches (15 to 20 cm) of water into the container. Freeze the water, either outdoors, if it is very cold, or in the freezer.

BRRR

BRRR

2 Run some warm water on the container to loosen the ice block, so that you can slip it out.

3 Run warm water directly on the center of the ice block to make a hole big enough for the candle. If it is warm where you live, store the ice candleholder in the freezer until you are ready to use it. Wear mittens or gloves to carry the ice.

Put the ice candleholder on the porch at night and ask an adult to light the candle for you to remind you of the light that came into the world through Jesus.

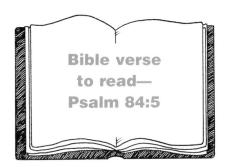

Bible verse to read— Psalm 84:5

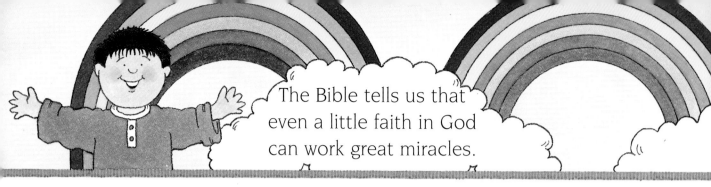

The Bible tells us that even a little faith in God can work great miracles.

Mustard Seed Necklace

you need:

 large-size wiggle eye

construction paper scrap

 mustard seed

thin gold cord

 white glue

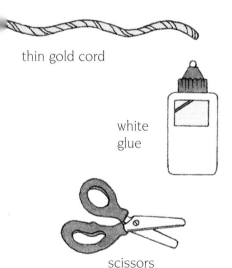
scissors

what you do:

1 Ask an adult to remove the back of a plastic wiggle eye so that you can use the clear plastic front.

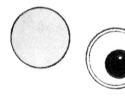

2 Trace around the eye on the construction paper and cut the tiny circle out.

3 Put glue all the way around the edge of the paper circle. Carefully set the mustard seed in the center of the circle. Glue on the clear plastic from the wiggle eye over the circle. Let the glue dry.

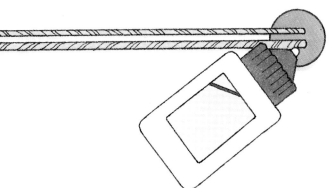

4 Cut a 2-foot (60-cm) length of gold cord. Glue the two ends of the cord to the back of the necklace to make a hanger.

When you wear the necklace, remember what the Bible tells us about faith as small as a mustard seed.

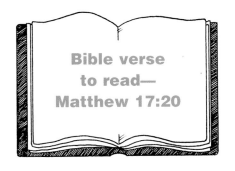

Bible verse
to read—
Matthew 17:20

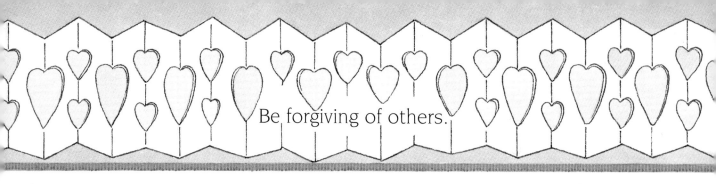

Be forgiving of others.

Forgiveness Bracelet

you need:

clear plastic
16-ounce
soda bottle

trim

sharp marker

construction
paper

scissors

yarn

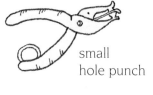
small
hole punch

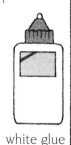
white glue

what you do:

1 If the bottle has a paper label on it, remove it. Ask an adult to cut off the top part of the bottle — the part where it slants in. Cut down the side of the remaining part of the bottle to the bottom. Cut two identical rings from the bottle, each about 1/2 inch (1.25 cm) wide.

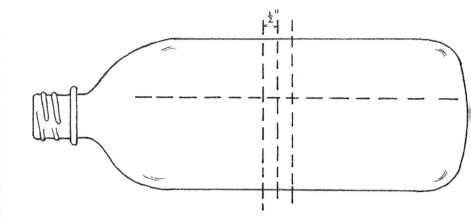

2 Cut a strip of construction paper the same size as the two rings.

Forgive and you will be forgiven. - Luke 6.37

3 Write a Bible verse about forgiveness on the paper, such as "Forgive and you will be forgiven" from the Book of Luke. Decorate the strip by gluing trim across the top and the bottom. Let the glue dry.

Forgive and you will be forgiven- Luke 6.37

4 Put the two plastic strips together with the paper strip in between them. Punch a hole at each end through all three layers.

5 Cut a 6-inch (15-cm) piece of yarn. Thread an end through each hole in the bracelet and tie the ends together, making the bracelet as large or small as you need it to be to slip it on over your hand.

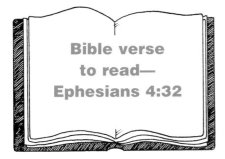

Wear this bracelet as a reminder to forgive others as God forgives you.

Bible verse to read— Ephesians 4:32

Do not worry, but rather
trust in God.

Lilies of the Field

you need:

white and green
construction paper

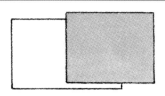

green and yellow
pipe cleaners

scissors

cellophane tape

pencil

what you do:

1 For each lily fold a piece of white construction paper in half. Use the pencil to trace the outline of your hand on the paper. Cut out the outline from the folded paper so that you have two hand shapes.

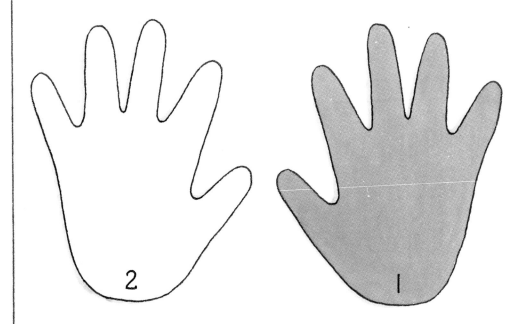

2 Trace your hand on the green construction paper. Cut out the hand shape.

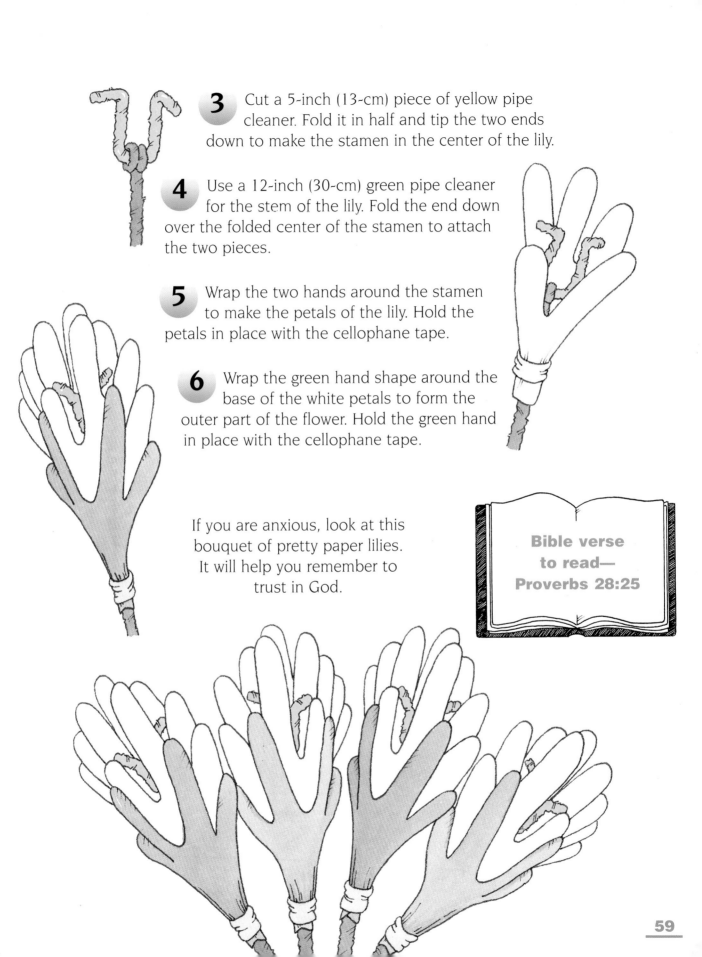

3 Cut a 5-inch (13-cm) piece of yellow pipe cleaner. Fold it in half and tip the two ends down to make the stamen in the center of the lily.

4 Use a 12-inch (30-cm) green pipe cleaner for the stem of the lily. Fold the end down over the folded center of the stamen to attach the two pieces.

5 Wrap the two hands around the stamen to make the petals of the lily. Hold the petals in place with the cellophane tape.

6 Wrap the green hand shape around the base of the white petals to form the outer part of the flower. Hold the green hand in place with the cellophane tape.

If you are anxious, look at this bouquet of pretty paper lilies. It will help you remember to trust in God.

Bible verse to read— Proverbs 28:25

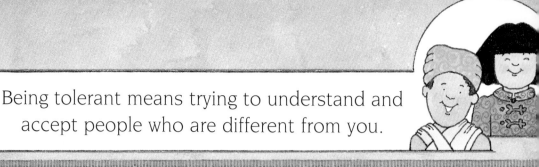

God's World Book

you need:

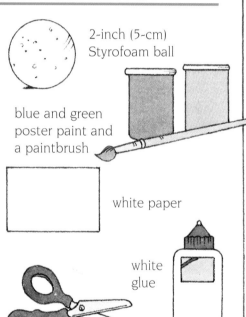

2-inch (5-cm) Styrofoam ball

blue and green poster paint and a paintbrush

white paper

white glue

scissors

thin ribbon

pictures from old magazines and catalogs of people from around the world

Styrofoam tray to work on

what you do:

1 Ask an adult to cut the Styrofoam ball in half. Paint the outside of both halves blue to look like the water on the Earth. Dab some green paint over the blue on each half to look like landforms. Let the two halves dry on the Styrofoam tray.

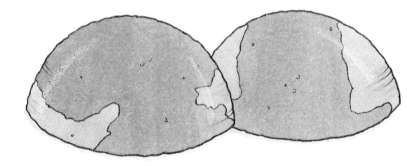

2 Trace around the flat end of one of the balls on the edge of the white paper.

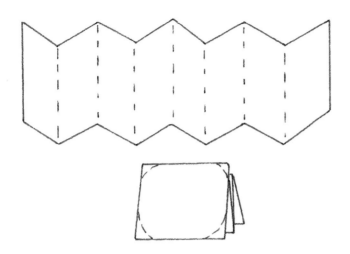

Fold the paper back and forth to make an accordion book the width of the circle. Cut around the top and bottom of the traced circle to make the accordion book fit between the two halves of the Styrofoam ball Earth.

3 Glue the back of the front page to the left side of the Earth and the last page to the right side of the Earth so that the two halves become the front and back cover of the accordion book.

4 Find pictures of God's people from around the world. Glue a different picture on each page of the book.

5 Close the book by tying the two halves of the Earth together with a ribbon.

Learn more about people who look or live in a way different from you.

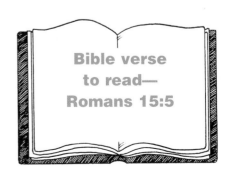

Bible verse to read— Romans 15:5

Cooperation means working together for the good of the group.

Cooperation Tulips

you need:

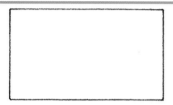

four large sheets of white construction paper

poster paint in green and four pretty colors and five paintbrushes

marker

three friends to work with you

newspaper to work on

what you do:

1 Each person should write his or her own name on the top of one paper.

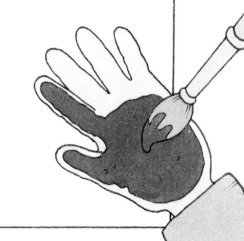

Michael

2 Each person should choose one color, besides green, to use. Each person needs to use a different color. The first person paints a hand with the chosen color, then, with fingers and thumb together, prints a hand tulip on the top left of each of the four papers. The hand may need to be repainted for each paper to get a good print.

3 The next person does the same thing, printing a hand tulip in the space next to the first one. Continue until each person has printed a tulip on each of the four papers. Everyone will need to wash their hands before continuing.

4 Each person may now go to his or her own paper and use the green paint to give each tulip a stem and some leaves.

5 Use the marker to write the name of the friend under the tulip that he or she printed.

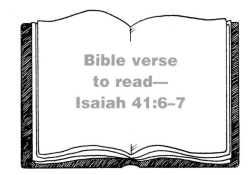

Bible verse to read—
Isaiah 41:6–7

Cooperating is such fun!

Michael

Michael   Kevin   Dave   Pat

About the Author and Illustrator

Twenty-five years as a teacher and director of nursery school programs has given Kathy Ross extensive experience in guiding young children through crafts projects. Among the many craft books she has written are CRAFTS FROM YOUR FAVORITE FAIRY TALES, THE BEST HOLIDAY CRAFTS EVER, CRAFTS FOR KIDS WHO ARE WILD ABOUT THE WILD, and CRAFTS FOR ALL SEASONS.

Sharon Lane Holm, a resident of Fairfield, Connecticut, won awards for her work in advertising design before shifting her concentration to children's books. Among the books she has illustrated recently are SIDEWALK GAMES AROUND THE WORLD, HAPPY BIRTHDAY, EVERYWHERE!, and HAPPY NEW YEAR, EVERYWHERE!, all by Arlene Erlbach, and BEAUTIFUL BATS by Linda Glaser.

Kathy Ross and Sharon Lane Holm have also collaborated on the earlier volume of this series, CRAFTS FROM YOUR FAVORITE BIBLE STORIES, as well as CHRISTMAS ORNAMENTS KIDS CAN MAKE, CHRISTMAS DECORATIONS KIDS CAN MAKE, MORE CHRISTMAS ORNAMENTS KIDS CAN MAKE, the popular Holiday Crafts for Kids series, and the Crafts for Kids Who Are Wild About series.